GUIDELINE ON CSR IMPLEMENTATION OVERSEAS

国家电网有限公司海外社会责任指南

STATE GRID CORPORATION OF CHINA

中国电力出版社
CHINA ELECTRIC POWER PRESS

U0874858

FOREWORD

前言

With sustainable development becoming a global focus, the Chinese government released the *Vision and Actions on Jointly Building Silk Road Economic Belt and 21st-Century Maritime Silk Road* in 2015, and China’s *National Plan on the Implementation of the 2030 Agenda for Sustainable Development* in 2016 to actively participate in the agenda of “the Belt and Road” for the sake of sustainable development around the world. Corporates of all countries have taken the implementation of corporate social responsibility (CSR) and the realization of sustainable development as important goals. In recent years, remarkable achievements have been made by State Grid Corporation of China (State Grid) in the operation and management of local institutions and operating entities along with important contributions to the economic and social development of the country or region where it operates. *State Grid Corporation of China Guideline on CSR Implementation Overseas* for Local institutions and Operating Entities (hereinafter referred to as the Guideline) is compiled for more effective management of the impact of its decisions and activities on the society, environment, and stakeholders in the country or region where it operates.

The Guideline consists of scope of application, background and objective, definitions and principles, management requirements, main topics and appendices, of which the “main topics” is an essential part for the implementation of CSR of State Grid, including corporate governance, environmental protection, energy services, safe operation, human rights and labor practices, community engagement and development, fair operating practices, and sustainable supply chain management.

To make the Guideline more scientific and applicable, in the preparation process the writers referred to Chinese and international standards and guidelines related to social responsibility and sustainable development, relevant international code of conduct, and the local laws and regulations, with due consideration given to the local operation of State Grid.

This Guideline, as the guiding document for local institutions and operating entities to implement corporate social responsibilities, is compiled and issued by State Grid who will be responsible for the subsequent improvements and revisions.

可持续发展已经成为全球关注的焦点，中国政府于 2015 年发布了《推动共建丝绸之路经济带和 21 世纪海上丝绸之路的愿景与行动》，于 2016 年出台了《中国落实 2030 年可持续发展议程国别方案》，主动参与到“一带一路”国家和全球可持续发展行动中。各国企业也都将履行社会责任、实现可持续发展作为重要目标。国家电网有限公司近年来在海外运营和管理中取得了显著成效，为运营所在地的经济社会发展作出了重要贡献。为了更加有效管理自身决策和活动对运营所在地的社会、环境和利益相关方造成的影响，国家电网有限公司（简称国家电网）编制了《国家电网有限公司海外社会责任指南》。

本指南包括适用范围、背景和目标、定义和原则、管理要求、主要议题、附录六个部分。其中主要议题是国家电网有限公司履行社会责任的重点内容，包括公司治理、环境保护、能源服务、安全运营、人权和劳工实践、社区参与和发展、公平运行实践、可持续供应链管理。

本指南在编制过程中，参照了国内外社会责任和可持续发展的相关标准、指南，考虑了相关国际行为规范和运营所在地法律法规要求，结合了公司海外运营实际，旨在保证《指南》的科学性和适用性。

本指南作为国家电网有限公司海外履行社会责任的指导性文件，由国家电网有限公司编制和发布，并负责后续的改进和修订。

CONTENTS

目录

Management Requirements
管理要求

Main Topics
主要议题

Appendices
附录

Scope of Application

适用范围

- The Guideline is formulated for the implementation of CSR and management activities of State Grid Corporation of China to help them with their business in accordance with relevant laws and regulations, international conventions, and other requirements that shall be observed.

- The Guideline contains established CSR codes of conduct but does not exhaust all the possible requirements of CSR. Users shall be responsible for correct application of the Guideline.

- The Guideline is applicable to all overseas institutions and operating entities of State Grid.

- When applying the Guideline, international code of conduct shall be respected, and the diversity of society, environment, law, culture, politics and organization in the countries and regions where State Grid operates, as well as the differences in economic conditions shall be fully considered.

- Compliance with the Guideline does not add or change the legal obligations or responsibilities of the implementer. In any case, State Grid shall first meet the requirements of local laws and regulations that are applicable, and apply more stringent requirements in cases where the laws and regulations coincide with the requirements of the Guideline.

- 本指南是对国家电网有限公司在海外履行社会责任以及开展相应管理活动的指导，帮助公司在海外根据相应的法律法规、国际公约和其他应当遵守的要求开展业务。

- 本指南包含确定的企业社会责任行为准则，但是并没有穷尽企业社会责任方面所有可能的要求，使用者必须对本指南的正确应用负责。

- 本指南以国家电网的所有海外机构及海外运营主体为适用对象。

- 在应用本指南时，应尊重国际行为规范，充分考虑运营所在地社会、环境、法律、文化、政治和组织的多样性，以及经济条件的差异性。

- 遵从本指南并不增加或改变指南实施者的法律义务或责任；在任何情况下，国家电网应首先满足适用的当地法律、法规的要求，并在法律法规与本指南要求重合的情况下适用其中更严格的要求。

Background and Objective

背景和目标

履责背景

Background of CSR Implementation

Objective requirement to practice the vision of a Community of Shared Future for Mankind

It has become a universal consensus to implement CSR. The corporate can achieve development and progress along with the global economy and community only when it fulfills corporate social responsibilities amid openness and development, advances international projects based on the principle of achieving shared growth and mutual benefit through discussion and collaboration, and moves deeper into the local society through methods such as market-oriented management, long-term management, localization, with practices of the vision of a Community of Shared Future for Mankind.

An inevitable choice to become a global corporate citizen

It is one of the major responsibilities of State Grid, a power supply corporation, to contribute to the global energy development. Focusing on "the Belt and Road" Initiative and promoting global energy interconnection, State Grid will give play to its comprehensive advantage to drive simultaneous development of the whole industrial chain and whole value chain, and well manage the social and environmental impacts brought by its operation. All these will contribute to the local economic and social development, as well as the management standards of State Grid on the way to becoming an excellent global corporate citizen.

Intrinsic requirements for active adaptation to the sustainable development trend

The Chinese government has made commitments to the implementation of the Sustainable Development Goals(SDGs) that aims to achieve a better and more sustainable future for all. State Grid will continue to follow and implement international CSR standards such as *ISO26000: 2010 Guidance on Social Responsibility* and the *Ten Principles of the UN Global Compact*, with active adaption to the trend and requirements of sustainable development for the realization of the Sustainable Development Goals.

Background of CSR Implementation

履责背景

践行人类命运共同体理念的客观需要

履行社会责任已经成为全球的普遍共识。国家电网有限公司只有在开放发展中履行企业社会责任，按照共商、共建、共享和互利共赢的原则推进国际化项目，坚持市场化经营、长期化经营、本土化经营，积极融入当地社会，以实际行动践行人类命运共同体理念，才能实现企业与全球经济社会的发展进步。

致力于成为全球企业公民的必然选择

作为电力能源供应企业，为全球能源发展贡献力量是国家电网有限公司的重要责任。公司聚焦“一带一路”建设，以推动构建全球能源互联网为重点，发挥综合优势，带动全产业链、全价值链的共同发展，有效管理自身运营给当地带来的社会和环境影响，不仅能够服务当地经济社会发展，而且能够提升公司的管理水平，成为优秀的全球企业公民。

主动适应可持续发展趋势的内在要求

联合国可持续发展目标（Sustainable Development Goals，SDGs）旨在倡导全球走向可持续发展之路。中国政府已经就落实联合国可持续发展目标作出了承诺。国家电网有限公司将持续遵守并践行 ISO26000: 2010《社会责任指南》、全球契约十项原则等国际社会责任标准，主动适应可持续发展的趋势和要求，以实际行动促进全球可持续发展目标的实现。

履责目标

Objectives of CSR Implementation

Benefit the local community with actions

In its operation and management practices,State Grid will in crease investment and promote local employment and economic development, with actions to improve conditions and social welfare for local community.

Create value through cooperation

In the process of local operation and management, State Grid will manage risks effectively, focus on closer cooperation with stakeholders, and work with the local community to solve problems and create value for common development.

Win recognition through communication

In the process of local operation and management, State Grid will strengthen communication with local stakeholders through various channels allowed by the local conditions to build harmonious relationships with stakeholders and to win their trust, recognition and support.

Objectives of CSR Implementation

履责目标

实践造福当地

通过在海外的运营和管理实践，加大对当地的投资，促进就业和经济发展，改善社区环境，用实际行动为当地增进社会福利。

合作创造价值

在海外运营和管理中，有效管理风险，注重加强与利益相关方的合作，共同寻求问题解决方案、创造价值，实现与当地的共同发展。

沟通赢得认同

在海外运营和管理中，通过各种符合当地实际的方式和途径，加强与当地利益相关方的沟通交流，营造和谐的利益相关方关系，努力赢得利益相关方的信任、认同与支持。

Definitions and Principles

定义和原则

履责内涵

Definition of CSR Implementation

Corporate social responsibility (CSR) refers to a corporate's efforts to maximize overall value and to ultimately promote the realization of sustainable development goals through effective management of the impacts of its decisions and activities on local stakeholders, society, and environment with transparent and ethical conduct.

Definition of CSR Implementation

履责内涵

企业社会责任指企业通过透明和道德的行为，有效管理自身的决策和活动对当地利益相关方、社会和环境的影响，努力追求综合价值最大化，最终促进可持续发展目标的实现。

基本原则

Basic Principles

Respect the rule of law

Respect for the rule of law is the bottom line of CSR implementation. State Grid shall fully understand the legal requirements of the country and community where it operates, with strict observation in the process of operation in order to prevent the illegal activities.

Respect international code of conduct

Respect for international code of conduct is critical to the success of local operation and management.State Grid shall be familiar with and understand the international code of conduct in local operation; in the case where laws are absent or inadequate, efforts should be made to respect international code of conduct; in the case where national and local laws in the place of operation conflict with international code of conduct, the latter shall be respected to the greatest possible extent.

Respect local culture

Respect for local culture is a necessary factor in local operation and management.State Grid shall understand and respect local cultural differences in history, ethnicity, religion, language, customs, etc., and take the initiative to avoid cultural conflicts in the process of operation.

Basic Principles

基本原则

尊重法治

尊重法治是应履行的底线责任。要充分了解运营所在地的国家及地方法律要求，在运营过程中严格遵照执行，坚决杜绝违法行为发生。

尊重国际行为规范

尊重国际行为规范关系到海外运营和管理的成败。应熟悉和了解海外运营所涉及的相关国际行为规范；在运营所在地没有法律或法律不健全的情况下，应努力尊重国际行为规范；在运营所在地的国家及地方法律与国际行为规范存在冲突的情况下，应最大可能地尊重国际行为规范。

尊重当地文化

尊重当地文化是海外运营和管理要考虑的必要因素。要了解并尊重当地的历史、民族、宗教、语言、风俗等文化差异，主动融入其中，避免在运营过程中产生文化冲突。

Respect stakeholder interests

Respect for stakeholder interests is also crucial to local operation and management. State Grid shall accurately identify the stakeholders associated with its activities and decision-making, with due respect for, consideration of, and timely response to their demands and expectations, and strive to win their understanding and recognition through win-win cooperation.

Abide by ethical standard

Ethical behavior is fundamental to local operation and management. State Grid shall abide by and uphold business ethics with integrity, and make decision-making and activities in the process of operation conform to ethical standards.

Adhere to transparent operation

Transparency is an important driver for local operation and management. State Grid shall make timely and effective information disclosure on governance, policies, systems, and decision-making that have impacts on the society, environment, and stakeholders, and promote communication and exchanges under the supervision of stakeholders.

Persist in continuous improvement

It is a necessary requirement to make continuous improvement in local operation and management. State Grid shall improve the effectiveness of operation and management through continuous improvement of its approaches to decision-making and activities so as to achieve sustainable development.

尊重利益相关方的利益

尊重利益相关方的利益是海外运营和管理的关键。要精准识别自身活动和决策涉及的利益相关方，尊重、考虑和回应其诉求和期望，努力实现与利益相关方的合作共赢，赢得理解与认同。

合乎道德

合乎道德是海外运营和管理的基础。要遵守商业道德、秉持商业伦理，诚实守信，运营过程中的决策和活动要符合道德标准。

坚持透明运营

坚持透明运营是海外运营和管理的重要驱动力。要及时有效地披露对社会、环境和利益相关方有影响的治理、政策、制度、决策等信息，促进沟通交流，自觉接受利益相关方监督。

坚持持续改进

坚持持续改进是海外运营和管理可持续的必然要求。要持续改进自身决策和活动的方式，提高运营管理的有效性，实现可持续发展。

Management Requirements

管理要求

尽责审查

Due Diligence

Due diligence refers to the prerequisite work that analyzes and determines the actual and potential impacts of corporate decisions and activities on the economy, society and environment to minimize negative consequences, through which State Grid can understand the objects and scope of operation and determine the content and boundary of its social responsibility.

Factors should be considered in due diligence include the national context in which State Grid operates, the actual and potential impacts of operation, and possible negative consequences from the actions of other entities or individuals closely related to activities of State Grid.

Due Diligence

尽责审查

尽责审查是分析、确定企业决策和活动对经济、社会、环境的实际与潜在影响，使消极影响最小化的前置性工作。通过尽责审查可以了解自身经营活动所影响的对象和范围，确定自身社会责任内容和边界。

在尽责审查中需要考虑的因素包括：经营所在地的国家背景、自身经营活动产生的实际和潜在的影响，以及与企业活动有密切联系的其他实体或个人的行动造成消极后果的可能性。

国家电网有限公司海外履行社会责任管理要求

Figure Management requirements for the implementation of CSR

实质性议题分析

Materiality Analysis

Materiality analysis issues underlines the content, procedures and methods of CSR implementation. In local operation and management, State Grid shall identify and prioritize material topics based on the external conditions for its decisions and activities and the impacts on local community, environment and stakeholders to provide the basis for future decisions and activities.

Materiality Analysis

实质性议题分析

实质性议题分析是决定海外履行社会责任的内容、程序和方式的基础。在海外运营和管理中，要根据自身决策和活动面临的外部环境，以及对当地社会、环境和利益相关方造成的影响，进行实质性议题的识别和排序，为下一步的决策和活动提供依据。

☆ 实质性议题分析矩阵

☆ Materiality analysis matrix

风险识别与评估

Risk Identification and Evaluation

Risk identification and evaluation are important safeguards for local operation and management.State Grid shall make careful analysis, identification and evaluation of the risks faced by its decisions and activities, especially social and environmental risks, and minimize the probability of occurrence or losses through risk measurement, evaluation, response and management, implementation, supervision and improvement.

Risk management mainly covers risk identification, risk analysis, risk evaluation and risk response.

☆ Risk management processes and methods

B Risk identification

- B_1 Business process decomposition
- B_2 Risk point identification
- B_3 Risk point numeration

A Risk response

- A_1 Risk aversion
- A_2 Risk sharing
- A_3 Risk control
- A_4 Risk acceptance

C Risk analysis

- C_1 Analysis of risk conditions
- C_2 Analysis of objects affected by risks
- C_3 Analysis of risk consequences

D Risk evaluation

- D_1 Risk evaluation and classification
- D_2 Risk hazard assessment
- D_3 Risk probability assessment

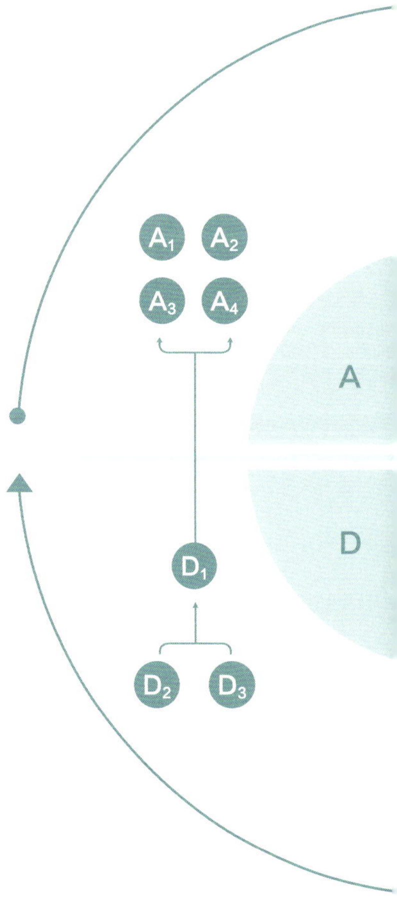

Risk Identification and Evaluation

风险识别与评估

风险识别和评估是海外运营和管理的重要保障。要认真分析、识别和评估决策及活动面临的各种风险，尤其是社会和环境风险。通过对风险的量度、评估、应对、管理执行和监督改进等手段，将风险发生的可能性或造成的损失降到最低。

风险管理主要包括风险识别、风险分析、风险评估、风险应对四个方面。

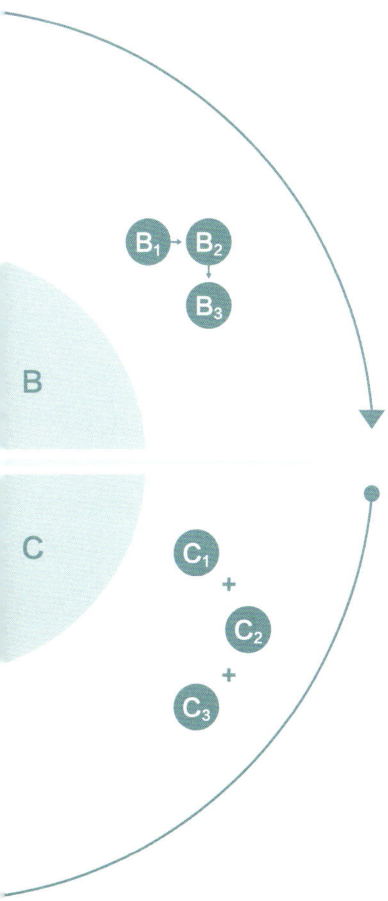

A 风险应对

- A1 风险规避
- A2 风险分担
- A3 风险控制
- A4 风险接受

B 风险识别

- B1 业务流程分解
- B2 风险点识别
- B3 风险点编号

D 风险评估

- D1 风险评估定级
- D2 风险危害评估
- D3 风险概率评估

C 风险分析

- C1 风险发生条件分析
- C2 风险影响对象分析
- C3 风险发生后果分析

☆ 风险管理过程和方法

最高管理者承诺

Top Management Commitment

Top management commitment determines the direction of the goals, aspirations and measures of local operation and management, through which State Grid will ensure a sound management system, the possible resource accessibility, the timely implementation, the objective performance evaluation as well as the effective consensus on engagement and cooperation. Top management commitment shall be disclosed publicly through social responsibility reports or other means accept the stakeholders' inspection on its implementation.

Top Management Commitment

最高管理者承诺

最高管理者承诺决定了海外运营和管理目标、愿望、行动的方向。通过最高管理者的承诺，确保管理体系的科学性、资源获得的可能性、实施执行的时效性、绩效评价的客观性、参与合作的共识有效性。最高管理者承诺应通过社会责任报告等方式公开披露，并接受利益相关方对承诺兑现情况的检验。

利益相关方参与

Stakeholder Engagement

Stakeholder engagement is a key element to be considered in local operation and management. State Grid shall first identify the types of stakeholders related to its decision-making activities and understand their expectations and demands to actively promote stakeholder engagement in the whole process of operation and management, supporting the implementation of strategic objectives, continuous improvement in the management system as well as sound and effective decision-making.

State Grid shall establish a mechanism for the effective engagement of important stakeholders in major projects and decision-making processes based on understanding and trust, and seek shared aspirations with active measures.

Stakeholder Engagement

利益相关方参与

利益相关方参与是海外运营和管理中要考虑的关键要素。应首先识别与自身决策活动相关的利益相关方类型，了解其期望和诉求，积极推进利益相关方参与经营管理全过程，为战略目标实施、管理体系持续改进、决策的科学性和有效性等提供支持。

应当建立重要项目和重大决策过程中关键利益相关方有效参与的机制，以理解和信任为基础，寻求共同目标，并采取积极措施予以实现。

信息披露

Information Disclosure

Information disclosure is an important way to improve the transparency of local operation and management. State Grid shall establish and improve its information disclosure mechanism for the timely, accurate and comprehensive disclosure of information and performance to stakeholders for better understanding. Information disclosure can be achieved through methods that include but are not limited to annual report, social responsibility report or sustainability report, local and foreign publications as well as media, along with channels such as official corporate websites, social networks and special communication activities.

Information Disclosure

信息披露

信息披露是提升海外运营和管理透明度的重要方式。应建立并不断完善企业信息披露机制，及时、准确、全面地向利益相关方披露信息和绩效，增进了解、赢得理解。信息披露的方式包括但不限于年报、社会责任报告或可持续发展报告、内外刊物、媒体等，也可以通过企业官方网站、社交网络、专项沟通活动等渠道进行。

问责与改进提升

Accountability and Improvement

Accountability and improvement are important measures for the achievement of sustainable development goals. State Grid shall establish and improve its supervision and assessment mechanism, and regularly evaluate the effectiveness of its social responsibility management mechanism.Analysis and evaluation on the impacts of decision-making activities on local cmmunity, environment and stakeholders also shall be conducted to identify and seize opportunities for improvement with proactive measures, which will continuously improve the local management and practical performance.

Accountability and Improvement

问责与改进提升

问责与改进提升是实现海外可持续发展目标的重要举措。要建立和完善监督考评机制，定期评估社会责任管理机制的有效性，分析评估决策活动对当地社会、环境和利益相关方造成的各种影响，识别并确定改进机会，采取改进措施，持续提升公司的海外管理和实践绩效。

Main Topics

主要议题

公司治理

Corporate Governance

Corporate governance refers to the system in which decisions are developed and implemented for the realization of sustainable development goals. It is the core function of a corporate as well as the internal decision-making framework.

Governance structure

In the process of local operation and management, State Grid shall establish and improve its governance structure based on the local external conditions and its operating practices to meet the needs of sustainable development.

Decision-making processes

In the process of local operation, State Grid shall establish sound, fair, transparent and effective decision-making processes based on the characteristics of its own decision-making activities to ensure the rationality and order of management and practice.

Management system

State Grid shall establish a sound management system and mechanism as an institutional guarantee for sustainable development in line with its decision-making procedures and specific practices.

Corporate Governance

公司治理

公司治理是指企业为实现可持续发展目标而制定和实施决策的系统，是企业的内部决策框架，也是企业的核心职能。

治理结构

海外运营和管理过程中，应根据当地的外部环境和自身实际，建立健全治理结构，以适应可持续发展的需要。

决策程序

在海外经营过程中，应根据自身决策活动的特点，建立科学、公正、透明、有效的决策程序，以保证管理和实践的合理有序。

管理制度

要根据自身的决策程序和具体实践，建立健全相应的管理制度，形成完善的管理机制，为国家电网可持续发展提供制度保障。

环境保护

Environmental Protection

Environmental protection refers to effective management of the impact of power grid construction and operation on the environment during operations in order to the sustainable development of resources and energy.

Pollution prevention

The operation of corporate may generate various forms of pollution and waste. State Grid shall act in compliance with local environmental laws and regulations and set up a strict management mechanism. With special funds for effective treatment of the pollutants and waste of various forms generated in operation, it shall promote the utilization of clean energy and develop new environmentally friendly technologies to minimize emissions.

Sustainable resource

State Grid shall prioritize the utilization of renewable resources, reduce the use of resources such as power, fuel, land, water, raw and processing materials, carry out technological innovations, and promote the recycling of resources and energy to avoid or reduce resource waste as much as possible.

Addressing climate change

The operation of corporate is directly or indirectly responsible for certain greenhouse gas emissions, and climate change also affects operation in some ways. State Grid shall deal with the impact of greenhouse gas emissions on climate change by formulating reasonable policies and taking specific actions.

Biodiversity protection

In the process of operation, State Grid shall consider the impact of its decisions and activities on the environment, biodiversity and natural habitats, take effective measures to avoid or reduce these impacts, and assume the responsibility for the consequences.

Environmental Protection

环境保护

环境保护是指在海外有效管理电网建设和运营过程中对环境的影响，促进资源和能源的可持续发展。

防止污染

企业运营可能会产生各种形式的污染和废弃物。应遵守当地的环保法律要求，制定严格的管理制度，提供专项资金，对污染物和废弃物进行有效处理，优先使用清洁能源，创新节能环保技术，减少排放。

资源可持续利用

最大限度地节约利用电力、燃料、原材料和加工材料、土地、水等资源，优先使用可再生资源，创新技术，促进能源资源的循环利用，尽可能地避免或减少资源浪费。

应对气候变化

企业运营对某些温室气体排放负有直接或间接的责任，同时气候变化也在以某些方式影响着企业运营。应制定相关政策并采取具体的行动以应对温室气体排放对气候变化带来的影响。

保护生物多样性

在运营过程中，要考虑决策和活动对环境、生物多样性和自然栖息地的影响，采取有效措施避免或降低这些影响，并对已经造成的影响承担责任。

能源服务

Energy Services

Energy services refer to secure and reliable energy supply for local economic and social development of the country or region where it operates.

Service quality

Staying customer-centered, State Grid should provide customers with convenient and high-quality energy services based on a sound service mechanism and unblocked customer service channels.

Protection of customer privacy

State Grid shall strictly restrict the types of customer information to be collected, standardize the way of collection and usage, and take appropriate measures to effectively protect customer privacy.

Sustainable consumption

State Grid encourages customers to save and rationally use energy and other resources by providing technical support, advocating the philosophy of sustainable development, etc.

Energy Services

能源服务

能源服务是指要为运营所在地提供保障可靠、可信赖的能源供应，服务当地经济社会发展。

服务质量

以客户为中心，通过建立优质服务机制，畅通客户服务渠道，为客户提供优质便捷的能源服务。

保护客户隐私

严格限制所收集客户信息的类型，规范信息获取和使用的方式，并采取妥善的保护措施，切实保护客户隐私。

可持续消费

通过提供技术支持、倡导可持续发展理念等方式，鼓励和引导客户节约、合理使用能源资源。

安全运营

Safe Operation

Safe operation means establish a sound work safety management system in accordance with the work safety requirements of the place where it operates and the actual operation practices to ensure the safety of people, equipment and society.

Personnel safety

State Grid shall ensure the safety of personnel and avoid personal casualty accidents through effective methods such as institutional arrangement, education, training, cultural development, etc.

Equipment safety

State Grid shall strengthen the safety management of equipment and facilities to ensure their healthy running.

Emergency management

State Grid shall establish a systematic pre-, in-, and post-event emergency management mechanism to minimize or reduce the occurrence of damage.

Safe Operation

安全运营

安全运营是指要根据运营所在地的安全生产要求和自身实际，建立健全安全生产管理体系，确保人身、设备和社会的安全。

人员安全

通过制度安排、教育培训、文化建设等多种途径和方式，保障人员的生命安全，避免人身伤亡事故的发生。

设备安全

加强对各种设备、设施的安全管理，确保设备设施健康运行。

应急管理

针对突发事件和紧急情况，应建立覆盖事前、事中、事后全过程的系统应急管理机制，最大限度地避免或减少损害的发生。

人权和劳工实践

Human Rights and Labor Practices

Human rights and labor practices mean that in local operation and management, State Grid shall act in strict compliance with the requirements of local laws and regulations as well as international code of conduct to safeguard the rights and interests of employees and create favorable working and living conditions for employees.

Elimination of discrimination

For employment, post arrangement and remuneration in the country or region where State Grid operates, employees shall not be treated differently due to their race, color, gender, religion or nationality.

Protection of rights and interests

State Grid shall protect the basic rights of employees, such as political rights, social rights and cultural rights.

Employee localization

State Grid shall hire as many local employees as possible in the country or region where it operates, so as to create more jobs for the local community.

Human Rights and Labor Practices

人权和劳工实践

人权和劳工实践是指在海外运营和管理中要严格遵照当地法律法规和国际行为规范中关于员工权益和权利的各项要求，为员工工作生活营造良好的环境。

杜绝歧视

在运营所在地雇佣员工、职位安排、薪酬待遇等方面，不能因种族、肤色、性别、宗教、民族等原因对员工进行区别对待。

保障权益

保障员工的政治权利、社会权利、文化权利等各项基本权利。

员工本地化

在运营所在地尽量多地雇佣当地员工，提供更多的就业机会。

Compensation and benefit

State Grid shall establish a sound compensation and benefit system based on the actual conditions of the place where it operates, and provide compensations not lower than the local minimum wage or the general standards of the local industry, on time and in full, and other welfare prescribed by local laws.

Career development

State Grid shall provide equal career development and training opportunities to all employees in the workplace through the establishment of a smooth promotion channel and systematic vocational skills training, and select, hire and retain the employees based on their comprehensive ability.

Occupational health

State Grid shall establish, implement and continuously improve the occupational health and safety management system to identify possible occupational health risks. It shall provide employees with the best occupational health and safety guarantee at work and take effective preventive measures to protect employees from harm.

Working conditions

State Grid shall create favorable working and living conditions for employees, make constant improvements based on the actual conditions of the workplace and the industry characteristics of the company; and care for the physical and mental health of employees so that they can focus on their work and live a happier life.

薪酬福利

根据运营所在地的实际情况，建立完善的薪酬福利体系，提供不低于当地最低工资标准或当地行业一般标准的薪酬，按时足额发放薪酬，并提供当地法律规定的各项福利保障。

职业发展

给予运营所在地所有员工平等的职业发展机会，建立畅通的职业晋升通道，提供系统的职业技能培训，依照员工的综合能力来选人、用人、留人。

职业健康

建立、实施并持续改进职业健康与安全管理体系，识别可能存在的职业健康风险，采取有效的防范措施保护员工远离危害，为员工提供最佳的职业健康与安全保障。

工作环境

结合运营所在地的实际情况和行业特点，为员工创造良好的工作和生活环境并不断改善，关爱员工的身心健康，让员工能够安心工作、快乐生活。

社区参与和发展

Community Engagement and Development

Community engagement and development mean that in local operation and management, State Grid shall provide necessary human, material and financial resources to the community to help solve problems, and actively participate in community building and the improvement of people's livelihood so as to achieve common development with the local community.

Promoting local employment

State Grid shall provide and create employment opportunities in accordance with local policy requirements and business practices, and contribute to poverty relief and economic and social development.

Education and culture

State Grid shall protect and promote culture and education in the country or region where it operates, and respect human rights so as to contribute to social cohesion and development.

Women and children

During operation and management, State Grid shall fully guarantee the rights of women and children, including the right to education, employment and participation in economic and social activities in local operation and management, without discrimination against women and children for any reason.

Community Engagement and Development

社区参与和发展

社区参与和发展是指在海外运营和管理中，通过为社区提供人力、物力和财力资源等支持，帮助社区解决问题，积极参与社区建设、改善民生，实现与当地社区的共同发展。

促进当地就业

按照当地政策要求和企业实际，为当地提供和创造就业机会，为减少贫困、促进经济与社会发展作出贡献。

教育和文化

在运营所在地保护并促进文化和教育，同时与尊重人权相互协调，对社会凝聚力和社会发展作出积极的影响。

妇女和儿童

在海外运营和管理中要充分保障妇女和儿童的权利，包括受教育、参加就业及参加经济和社会活动的权利，不能以任何理由歧视妇女和儿童。

Community health

State Grid shall respect the right to health and contribute to promoting community health, preventing health threats, and mitigating disease hazards in appropriate ways.

Community infrastructure

State Grid shall give full play to its industrial and professional advantages to support the construction of power, transportation, communications, drinking water, sanitation, and other public infrastructure projects.

Disaster relief and mitigation

State Grid shall offer support to community philanthropy through providing technology, services, donations and other assistance to facilitate the disaster prevention, relief and mitigation.

Community communication

State Grid shall pay attention to communication with local stakeholders to listen to their demands and expectations, through which they can have a deeper and more comprehensive understanding of State Grid and contribute to its development.

社区健康

尊重健康权，以适当的方式为促进社区健康、防范健康威胁、减轻疾病危害作出贡献。

社区基础设施

发挥行业优势和自身的专业优势，支持社区电力、交通、通信、饮水、卫生等公共基础设施建设。

救灾减灾

积极支持社区慈善事业，通过技术、服务和捐赠等多种形式，为社区防灾、救灾、减灾提供帮助。

社区沟通

重视与当地利益相关方的沟通交流，积极主动地了解利益相关方的诉求和期望，让当地利益相关方更加深入、全面地了解公司，进而支持公司的发展。

公平运行实践

Fair Operating Practices

Fair operating practice means follow the principle of equality, transparency, integrity and fairness co-cooperate with partners, suppliers, contractors, competitors, and industry organizations in a fair and responsible manner and ensure fair competition and orderly industrial development.

Anti-corruption and anti-commercial bribery

State Grid shall establish a management mechanism and accountability system to prevent and punish for commercial bribery and other corrupt practices in business and stakeholder relationships, and take necessary measures to protect the whistleblowers of commercial bribery and corruption.

Fair competition

State Grid shall actively involve itself in competition through constant improvement of technology and development of new technologies to enhance its own competitiveness and eliminate unfair competition.

Respect for property rights

State Grid shall respect and protect the tangible property rights, intellectual property rights and proprietary technologies of others, and guide people to respect the tangible property rights, intellectual property rights and proprietary technologies to promote and inspire creativity and innovation.

公平运行实践是指坚持平等、透明、诚信、公正的原则，公平、负责地与合作伙伴、供应商、承包商、竞争者及行业组织等进行合作，并引导其进行公平竞争，维护行业发展秩序。

Fair Operating Practices

公平运行实践

反腐败与反商业贿赂

建立管理机制和责任制度，预防和惩治在商业经营和利益相关方关系中的商业贿赂和其他腐败行为，并采取必要措施对商业贿赂和腐败行为的举报人给予保护。

公平竞争

积极参与竞争，不断改进技术、开发新技术，提升自身的竞争力，坚决杜绝不正当竞争行为。

尊重产权

尊重和保护他人的有形产权、知识产权和专有技术，并引导他人尊重企业自身的有形产权、知识产权和专有技术，以促进和激励创造与创新精神。

可持续供应链管理

Sustainable Supply Chain Management

Sustainable supply chain management means promote local and foreign suppliers as well as the whole supply chain to implement social responsibility and pursue sustainable development through cooperation and communication with all parties of the supply chain.

Supplier review

State Grid shall evaluate and review suppliers in accordance with the requirements of social responsibility standards to avoid social and environmental risks.

Responsible procurement

In terms of procurement strategy, State Grid shall consider the environmental, social and ethical performance of products or services to be procured throughout the life cycle. Whenever possible, it shall give preference to the products and services that minimize the environmental and social impacts, and prioritize the procurement of local products and services in the first place when possible.

Equal cooperation

In local operation and management, State Grid shall advocate equal, voluntary, open and transparent cooperation with suppliers for win-win development.

Sustainable Supply Chain Management

可持续供应链管理

可持续供应链管理是指要促进国内外供应商及整个供应链履行社会责任，通过与供应链各方的协作、沟通，共同追求可持续发展。

供应商审查

在选择供应商时要按照社会责任标准要求对其进行评估和审查，避免社会和环境风险的发生。

负责任采购

在采购策略中应考虑拟采购的产品或服务在整个生命周期中的环境、社会和道德绩效。如有可能，应优先选择环境和社会影响最小化的产品和服务，优先选择运营所在地的产品和服务。

平等合作

在海外运营和管理中应坚持与供应商的平等、自愿、公开、透明合作，实现共赢发展。

Appendices

附录

术语

Terms

Corporate social responsibility

The responsibility of a corporate for the impacts of its decisions and activities on society and the environment, through transparent and ethical behavior that

- contributes to sustainable development, including health and the welfare of society;
- takes into account the expectations of stakeholders;
- is in compliance with applicable law and consistent with international code of conduct;
- and is integrated throughout the organization and practiced in its relationships.

* Activities include products, services and procedures.
Relationships refer to the activities of a corporate within its impact.
Responsibilities assumed involve the responsibility attached to the product or service and the responsibility for the realization of the product or service.

Stakeholder

Any individual or group that has an interest in any decision or activity of a corporate.

Stakeholder engagement

Any activity undertaken to create opportunities for dialogue between a corporate and one or more of its stakeholders, with the aim of providing an informed basis for the corporate's decisions.

Terms

术语

企业社会责任

企业通过透明和道德的行为，为其决策和活动对社会和环境的影响而承担的责任。这些行为如下：

- 致力于可持续发展，包括健康和社会福祉；
- 考虑利益相关方的期望；
- 遵守适用法律，并符合国际行为规范；
- 融入整个企业并在其关系中得到践行。

* 活动包括产品、服务和过程。
关系是指企业在其影响范围内的活动。
承担的责任包括附着在产品或服务上的责任和产品或服务实现过程中的责任。

利益相关方

在企业的决策或活动中有利益的个人或团体。

利益相关方参与

为创造企业与一个或多个利益相关方的对话机会而开展的活动，目的是为企业决策提供信息基础。

Sustainable development

Development that meets the needs of the present without compromising the ability of future generations to meet their own needs.

☆ Sustainable development is about integrating the goals of a high quality of life, health and prosperity with social justice and maintaining the earth's capacity to support life in all its diversity. These social, economic and environmental goals are interdependent and mutually reinforcing. Sustainable development can be treated as a way of expressing the broader expectations of society as a whole.

Environment

Natural surroundings in which an organization operates, including air, water, land, natural resources, flora, fauna, people, outer space and their interrelationships.

Community

A community is a social group that shares common consciousness and interests in the same geographical area. This area can be as small as a village, or as large as a country, or even the whole planet.

Transparency

Openness about decisions and activities that affect society, the economy and the environment, and willingness to communicate these in a clear, accurate, timely, honest and complete manner.

Supplier

Corporates and their subsidiaries as well as individual industrial and commercial enterprises, including manufacturers, distributors and other intermediaries that provide products and/or services directly to the corporate.

可持续发展

既满足当代人需要又不危及后代人，又满足其需要的能力的发展。

☆ 可持续发展事关高品质生活、健康、繁荣等目标与社会公正的融合，以及维护地球支撑生物多样性的能力。这些社会、经济和环境目标是相互依存和相辅相成的。可持续发展可被视为全社会更广泛期望的一种表达方式。

环境

企业运行所处的自然环境，包括空气、水、土地、自然资源、植物、动物、人和太空及其相互关系。

社区

社区是生活在同一地理区域内、具有共同意识和共同利益的社会群体，这个区域可小至村庄大至国家乃至整个地球。

透明度

影响社会、经济和环境的决策和活动的公开性，以及以清晰、准确、及时、诚实和完整的方式进行沟通的意愿。

供应商

直接向企业提供商品及服务的企业及其分支机构、个体工商户，包括制造商、经销商和其他中介商等。

Fair competition

Open, equal and fair competition among competitors in the same market that does not impair the interests of their respective stakeholders for comparative advantage, with each competitor accepting the role and judgment of value law and survival of the fittest, and independently bearing the result of competition.

Commercial bribery

Any act of paying money or property with absence of consideration or false consideration or other means to bribe the other party or individual in order to sell or purchase products or services. The act of employees selling or purchasing products or services by means of commercial bribery belongs to the act of commercial bribery.

Corporate social responsibility report

Corporate social responsibility report is a specific report that a corporate, based on the need for social responsibility communication with stakeholders, organizes regular or irregular public release of its social responsibility concept and understanding, and systematically discloses its social responsibility activities and performance information.

Social responsibility communication

Social responsibility communication refers to the dialogue and communication between a corporate and stakeholders through socialized expression, with the intention to promote the comprehension, understanding and trust between the corporate and different stakeholders, and to create a favorable internal and external development environment.

公平竞争

处于同一市场条件下的各个竞争者之间进行的，不以损害各自利益相关方利益作为比较优势的公开、平等、公正的竞争。各个竞争者共同接受价值规律和优胜劣汰的作用与评判，并各自独立承担竞争的结果。

商业贿赂

企业为销售或购买产品和服务而采用无对价或对价虚假地给付财物或以其他手段贿赂交易对方或个人的行为。员工采用商业贿赂手段为其销售或购买产品和服务的行为属于商业贿赂行为。

企业社会责任报告

社会责任报告是企业基于与利益相关方进行社会责任沟通的需要，组织定期或不定期对外公开发布的一种展示其社会责任理念和认识，并系统披露其社会责任活动及其绩效信息的特定报告。

社会责任沟通

社会责任沟通是企业通过社会化的表达方式与利益相关方开展的对话和交流，促进企业与不同利益相关方之间的了解、理解和信任，营造良好的内外部发展环境。

编制依据

References

International conventions and social responsibility-related documents

- United Nations (UN): *Universal Declaration of Human Rights*, 1948
- United Nations (UN): *International Covenant on Civil and Political Rights*, 1966
- United Nations (UN): *International Covenant on Economic, Social and Cultural Rights*, 1966
- United Nations (UN): *Convention on the Elimination of All Forms of Discrimination against Women*, 1979
- United Nations (UN): *Convention on the Rights of the Child*, 1989
- United Nations (UN): *Convention on the Rights of Persons with Disabilities*, 2006
- International Labor Organization (ILO): *Weekly Rest (Industry) Convention*, 1921 (No. 14)
- International Labour Organization (ILO): *Equality of Treatment (Accident compensation) convention* 1925, (No. 19)
- International Labor Organization (ILO): *Convention Concerning the Creation of Minimum Wage-Fixing Machinery*, 1928 (No. 26)
- International Labour Organization (ILO): *Minimum Age Convention* (Revised), 1937 (No. 59)
- International Labour Organization (ILO): *Equal Remuneration Convention*, 1951 (No. 100)
- International Labour Organization (ILO): *Discrimination (Employment and Occupation) Convention*, 1958 (No.111)
- International Labor Organization (ILO): *Employment Policy Convention*, 1964 (No. 122)
- International Labour Organization (ILO): *Minimum Age Convention*, 1973 (No. 138)
- International Labour Organization (ILO): *Tripartite Consultation (International Labour Standards) Convention*, 1976 (No. 144)
- International Labour Organization (ILO): *Labor Administration Convention*, 1978 (No. 150)
- International Labour Organization (ILO): *Occupational Safety and Health Convention*, 1981 (No. 155)
- International Labour Organization (ILO): *Vocational Rehabilitation and Employment (Disabled Persons) Convention*, 1983 (No. 159)
- International Labour Organization (ILO): *Chemicals Convention*, 1990 (No. 170)
- International Labour Organization (ILO): *Worst Forms of Child Labour Convention*, 1999 (No. 182)
- *Stockholm Convention on POPs*
- *Montreal Protocol on Substances that Deplete the Ozone Layer (Montreal Protocol)*
- United Nations (UN): *UN Framework Convention on Climate Change*, 1992
- United Nations (UN): *Kyoto Protocol to the United National Framework Convention and Climate Change*, 1997
- *Paris Convention for the Protection of Industrial Property*
- *Universal Copyright Convention*
- United Nations (UN): *Convention against Corruption*, 2005
- *The Ten Principles of the UN Global Compact*
- ISO 26000: 2010 *Guidance on social responsibility*
- Global Reporting Initiative (GRI): *Sustainability Reporting Guidelines Version 4.0 (G4)*
- ISO 9001: 2015 *Quality management systems — Requirements*
- ISO 14001: 2014 *Environmental management systems — Requirements with guidance for use*
- OHSAS 18001: 2007 *Occupational health and safety management systems requirements*

References

编制依据

国际公约和国际社会责任相关文件

- 《世界人权宣言》
- 《公民和政治权利国际公约》
- 《经济、社会及文化权利国际公约》
- 《消除对妇女一切形式歧视公约》
- 《儿童权利公约》
- 《残疾人权利公约》
- 《工业企业中实行每周休息公约》（国际劳工组织公约第 14 号）
- 《事故赔偿同等待遇公约》（国际劳工组织公约第 19 号）
- 《制定最低工资确定办法公约》（国际劳工组织公约第 26 号）
- 《最低年龄公约（修正）》（国际劳工组织公约第 59 号）
- 《同酬公约》（国际劳工组织公约第 100 号）
- 《消除就业和职业歧视公约》（国际劳工组织公约第 111 号）
- 《就业政策公约》（国际劳工组织公约第 122 号）
- 《准予就业最低年龄公约》（国际劳工组织公约第 138 号）
- 《国际劳工标准三方协商公约》（国际劳工组织公约第 144 号）
- 《劳动行政管理公约》（国际劳工组织公约第 150 号）
- 《职业安全和卫生及工作环境公约》（国际劳工组织公约第 155 号）
- 《残疾人职业康复和就业公约》（国际劳工组织公约第 159 号）
- 《化学品公约》（国际劳工组织公约第 170 号）
- 《最恶劣形式的童工劳动公约》（国际劳工组织公约第 182 号）
- 《关于持久性有机污染物的斯德哥尔摩公约》
- 《关于消耗臭氧层物质的蒙特利尔议定书》
- 《联合国气候变化框架公约》及《京都议定书》
- 《保护工业产权巴黎公约》
- 《世界版权公约》
- 《联合国反腐败公约》
- 《联合国全球契约十项原则》
- ISO 26000: 2010《社会责任指南》
- 《全球报告倡议组织可持续发展报告指南（4.0 版）》
- ISO 9001: 2015《质量管理体系》
- ISO 14001: 2004《环境管理体系规范及使用指南》
- OHSAS 18001: 2007《职业健康与安全管理体系规范》

Relevant laws and regulations as well as social responsibility-related documents in China

- *Constitution of the People's Republic of China and all amendments to the Constitution*
- *Labor Law of the People's Republic of China*
- *Labor Contract Law of the People's Republic of China*
- *Employment Promotion Law of the People's Republic of China*
- *Trade Union Law of the People's Republic of China*
- *Law of the People's Republic of China on the Protection of Rights and Interests of Women*
- *Law of the People's Republic of China on the Protection of Minors*
- *Law of the People's Republic of China on the Protection of Disabled Persons*
- *Work Safety Law of the People's Republic of China*
- *Law of the People's Republic of China on the Prevention and Control of Occupational Diseases*
- *Labor Disputes Mediation and Arbitration Law of the People's Republic of China*
- *Environmental Protection Law of the People's Republic of China*
- *Water Pollution Prevention and Control Law of the People's Republic of China*
- *Atmospheric Pollution Prevention and Control Law of the People's Republic of China*
- *Law of the People's Republic of China on Prevention and Control of Environmental Pollution Caused by Solid Wastes*
- *Law of the People's Republic of China on Prevention and Control of Pollution from Environmental Noise*
- *Law of the People's Republic of China on Environmental Impact Assessment*
- *Law of the People's Republic of China on Promoting Clean Production*
- *Energy Conservation Law of the People's Republic of China*
- *Renewable Energy Law of the People's Republic of China*
- *Circular Economy Promotion Law of the People's Republic of China*
- *Product Quality Law of the People's Republic of China*
- *Law of the People's Republic of China on Protection of Consumer Rights and Interests*
- *Anti-Unfair Competition Law of the People's Republic of China*
- *Science and Technology Progress Law of the People's Republic of China*

中国政府相关法律和社会责任相关文件

- 《中华人民共和国宪法》及历次宪法修正案
- 《中华人民共和国劳动法》
- 《中华人民共和国劳动合同法》
- 《中华人民共和国就业促进法》
- 《中华人民共和国工会法》
- 《中华人民共和国妇女权益保障法》
- 《中华人民共和国未成年人保护法》
- 《中华人民共和国残疾人保障法》
- 《中华人民共和国安全生产法》
- 《中华人民共和国职业病防治法》
- 《中华人民共和国劳动争议调解仲裁法》
- 《中华人民共和国环境保护法》
- 《中华人民共和国水污染防治法》
- 《中华人民共和国大气污染防治法》
- 《中华人民共和国固体废物污染环境防治法》
- 《中华人民共和国环境噪声污染防治法》
- 《中华人民共和国环境影响评价法》
- 《中华人民共和国清洁生产促进法》
- 《中华人民共和国节约能源法》
- 《中华人民共和国可再生能源法》
- 《中华人民共和国循环经济促进法》
- 《中华人民共和国产品质量法》
- 《中华人民共和国消费者权益保护法》
- 《中华人民共和国反不正当竞争法》
- 《中华人民共和国科学技术进步法》

- *Anti-Monopoly Law of the People's Republic of China*
- *Patent Law of the People's Republic of China*
- *Trademark Law of the People's Republic of China*
- Ministry of Human Resources and Social Security of the People's Republic of China:*Provisions on Collective Contract (No.22)*
- *State Council of the People's Republic of China: Provisions on the Prohibition of Using Child Labor (No.364)*
- Ministry of Human Resources and Social Security of the People's Republic of China: *Provisions on Special Protection for Minor Workers,1994 (No.498)*
- State Council of the People's Republic of China: *Regulation on the Employment of the Disabled(No.488)*
- Ministry of Human Resources and Social Security of the People's Republic of China: *Approval Process of the Implement of Flexible Working Hour System and the Working Hour System of Comprehensive Calculation,1994 (No.503)*
- State Council of the People's Republic of China: *Regulation on Public Holidays for National Annual Festivals and Memorial Days (No.644)*
- State Council of the People's Republic of China: *State Council's decision to make amendments to the State Council on Working Hours of Workers and Staff (No.174)*
- State Council of the People's Republic of China: *Regulations on Paid Annual Leave for Employees (No.514)*
- Ministry of Human Resources and Social Security of the People's Republic of China: *Provisions on Minimum Wages (No.21)*
- State Council of the People's Republic of China: *Regulations on the Reporting, Investigation and Disposition of Work Safety Accidents (No.453)*
- State Council of the People's Republic of China: *Regulation on Work-Related Injury Insurance (No.586)*
- Ministry of Commerce of the People's Republic of China: *Administration Measures for the Recovery of Renewable Resources,2007 (No.8)*
- State Administration of Industry and Commerce of the People's Republic of China: *Interim Provisions on Banning Commercial Bribery (No.82)*
- GB/T 36000 — 2015 *Guidance on social responsibility*
- GB/T 36001 — 2015 *Guidance on social responsibility reporting*
- GB/T 36002 — 2015 *Guidance on classifying social responsibility performance*
- State-Owned Assets Supervision and Administration Commission of the State Council ,National Development and Reform Commission and Ministry of Finance of the People's Republic of China: *Guidelines to the State-owned Enterprises Directly under the Central Government on Fulfilling Corporate Social Responsibilities, 2008 (No.1)*
- State-Owned Assets Supervision and Administration Commission of the State Council ,National Development and Reform Commission and Ministry of Finance of the People's Republic of China: *The 12th Five-Year Plan Harmony Development Strategy Implementation Summary of Central Enterprises,2011(No.146)*
- *Guidelines to the State-owned Enterprises on Better Fulfilling Corporate Social Responsibilities*
- *Guidelines on Social Responsibility for Chinese Industrial Enterprises and Industrial Associations,2015*

- 《中华人民共和国反垄断法》
- 《中华人民共和国专利法》
- 《中华人民共和国商标法》
- 《集体合同规定》（劳动和社会保障部令第 22 号）
- 《禁止使用童工规定》（国务院令第 364 号）
- 《未成年工特殊保护规定》（劳部发［1994］498 号）
- 《残疾人就业条例》（国务院令第 488 号）
- 《关于企业实行不定时工作制和综合计算工时工作制的审批方法》（劳部发［1994］503 号）
- 《全国年节及纪念日放假办法》（国务院令第 644 号）
- 《国务院关于职工工作时间的规定》（国务院令第 174 号）
- 《职工带薪年休假条例》（国务院令第 514 号）
- 《最低工资规定》（劳动和社会保障部令第 21 号）
- 《生产安全事故报告和调查处理条例》（国务院令第 453 号）
- 《工伤保险条例》（国务院令第 586 号）
- 《再生资源回收管理办法》（商务部令［2007］第 8 号）
- 《关于禁止商业贿赂行为的暂行规定》（国家工商行政管理局令第 82 号）
- GB/T 36000—2015《社会责任指南》
- GB/T 36001—2015《社会责任报告编写指南》
- GB/T 36002—2015《社会责任绩效分类指引》
- 《关于中央企业履行社会责任的指导意见》（国资发研究［2008］1 号）
- 《中央企业“十二五”和谐发展战略实施纲要》（国资发研究［2011］146 号）
- 《关于国有企业更好履行社会责任的指导意见》
- 《中国工业企业社会责任管理指南（2015）》

图书在版编目（CIP）数据

国家电网有限公司海外社会责任指南 / 国家电网有限公司编 .— 北京：中国电力出版社，2018.11

ISBN 978-7-5198-2605-5

Ⅰ . ①国… Ⅱ . ①国… Ⅲ . ①电力工业 – 工业企业 – 社会责任 – 中国 – 指南 Ⅳ . ① F426.61-62

中国版本图书馆 CIP 数据核字（2018）第 246775 号

出版发行：中国电力出版社
地　　址：北京市东城区北京站西街 19 号（邮政编码 100005）
网　　址：http://www.cepp.sgcc.com.cn
责任编辑：周天琦（010—63412243）
责任校对：黄　蓓　常燕昆
装帧设计：北京大良造品牌顾问有限责任公司
责任印制：邹树群

印　刷：北京雅昌艺术印刷有限公司
版　次：2018 年 11 月第一版
印　次：2018 年 11 月北京第一次印刷
开　本：889 毫米 ×1194 毫米　16 开本
印　张：4.75 印张
字　数：144 千字
定　价：30.00 元

版 权 专 有　侵 权 必 究
本书如有印装质量问题，我社发行部负责退换